TRENDSETTER

BY SARAH STRONG

ILLUSTRATED BY MARY SANDERS

This book is dedicated to my two sons and every kid in the world who may one day question the way that they look. When you approach these moments in life, remember your greatest responsibility will always be to love yourself, even when the world says differently.

Kelly woke up as happy as she could be. After all, today was her first day of 5th grade! "Wow," she thought to herself, "summer really went by fast." Kelly jumped right out of bed and headed straight to the bathroom.

As she was walking down the hallway to the bathroom, she could smell the bacon her mother was frying.

"Good morning baby, are you ready for your first day of being a 5th grader?"

"Yes, ma'am but I'm a little nervous."

"No need to be nervous baby. You're going to be just fine. You know why?"

"Why, Mama? Because you're smart, beautiful, and kind. You can't go wrong with those three! Now go get ready for school."

After breakfast, Kelly walked back down the hallway and into the bathroom to brush her tiny white teeth with braces. Then she washed her face filled with light freckles. As Kelly looked in the mirror, she couldn't help but to notice how her hair had frizzed up overnight because her bonnet and scarf had come off. "Mommmmm!" she screamed at the top of her lungs with a crackle in her voice. "Look at my hair! Everyone is going to laugh at me," she said as a tear ran down her face.

As long as Kelly could remember, she had been wearing her hair straight down her back with no frizz. But Kelly's mom had recently decided to stop using perms due to the damage it was causing to Kelly's hair.

Kelly's mom came into the bathroom, looked at her with a smile, and said, "Baby, you're beautiful no matter how you wear your hair."

"But, Mom, I've always worn my hair straight for as long as I can remember, and now it looks nappy!"

"Baby girl, those are not naps. Those are your natural curls."

"But, Mom, I'm already wearing these braces that feel like they are squeezing every tooth in my mouth, and now my hair! This is going to be the worst first day of 5th grade because everyone is going to laugh at me."

Kelly's mom took her daughter's face into her hands.

"Kelly, let me tell you something: other's opinions about you are just that! Opinions! See, you have a special gift. You're beautiful on the inside and out! When you love yourself, how others feel about you doesn't matter one bit. Now, go in my room and grab my wide tooth comb, brush and hair gel."

Kelly ran into her mom's room, knowing she had less than an hour before the bus arrived.

Just a few minutes later, Kelly's mom had worked her magic. "All done baby girl, take a look!"

Kelly had kept her eyes closed as her mother did her hair, but when she opened her eyes, she couldn't believe what she was seeing! Her mother had taken her frizzy natural hair and braided two big braids to the back of her head and added in a few gold hair jewels. Kelly thought she looked like some sort of a goddess, but then instantly became nervous. "Mom, what do you think the other kids will think of my hair?"

"Listen to me, Kelly." Her mother's once gentle, soft-spoken tone became a loud stern voice that would make a whole room stand still. "Loving yourself isn't about what others think or following trends and what others are doing. When you love yourself, you set the trends and people may laugh in the beginning, but soon they will follow your lead. Now, go get dressed because your bus will be here in less than 20 minutes, and we all know Mrs. Willis does not wait on anyone!"

Kelly started to feel jitter bugs in her stomach. What was her best friend Hailee going to think? They always wore their hair straight and, after all, that was the trend for the most popular 5th graders. Kelly rushed into her room and quickly put on her clothes and shoes. As she looked in the mirror, she realized that her hair actually did look pretty cool, but what would the other kids on her bus and at school think?

"Kelly!" Her mom screamed, "The bus is pulling up!" As Kelly walked out of the room, her mom was standing at the door with her lunchbox. Her mom grabbed her tight into a hug and said, "Baby girl, you look as beautiful as ever. You go, girl, and remember you set the trend, never follow."

"Thanks, Mom!" Then Kelly hurried down out to the sidewalk where she met Hailee at the door of the bus.

"Wow," Hailee said with a frown, "What happened to your hair?"

Kelly instantly felt her stomach sink, but she said with confidence, "I decided to try something new! Do you like it?"

"No, I don't! We always wear our hair straight, remember?"

After they got on the bus, Hailee decided to sit with another girl in their grade whose hairstyle was more like Hailee's.

As Kelly made her way towards the back of the bus almost ready to burst into tears, a girl who she had never seen before looked up at her and asked if she would like to sit with her. Kelly said yes but as she was sitting down, she noticed this girl also had her hair straightened out with a fresh perm.

"My name is Olivia. What's yours?"

"Kelly."

"I'm new in town, and this is my first day of 5th grade."

"Mine, too."

"I really like your braids. Do they hurt?"

Kelly said, "No, my mom did them this morning because my hair started t—" But before she could finish, Olivia had her hands on Kelly's head. "Wow, I want my hair just like that, but my mom can't braid!"

"Well I'm sure my mom would do yours as well."

They continued to talk until they got to school, where Kelly discovered they were in the same class and so was Hailee!

As much as Kelly was enjoying talking to Olivia, she still couldn't believe her best friend wouldn't talk to her because her hair was different. As Kelly and Olivia made their way to into their class, they looked around to find desks with their names on them. Mrs. Appleberry , their homeroom teacher, greeted them and couldn't help but to notice Kelly 's braids. "Kelly, your hair is so pretty. Who did it?"

"My mom," Kelly said proudly and now with much more confidence. Her classmates started to chime in, stating how they loved Kelly's hair too! Kelly could see Hailee's head drop as if she were trying not to notice the compliments Kelly was receiving by their classmates.

As they let out for recess, a few girls from their class started to come up to Kelly and ask who did her hair. Soon they all began to play with each other, but Kelly couldn't help but notice Hailee all alone on the swings. She ran over and asked what was wrong.

"Hailee, are you okay? Did I do something wrong?"

"Oh yes, you most definitely did something wrong. You wore your hair differently than what we have always done!"

"But I didn't plan to do this. My mom didn't perm my hair this time and it was frizz—" Before she could finish, Hailee walked off. Kelly couldn't believe her best friend was acting in such a manner over something as small as hair! Kelly made her way back to play with Olivia and the rest of their classmates.

That afternoon when Kelly arrived home from school, her mom was in the kitchen preparing dinner. Best of all ,she was making Kelly's favorite, lasagna! "Kelly how was your day?"

"It was somewhat great. I love my new teacher, I made a new friend, and everyone seemed to really like my hair except for Hailee. She wouldn't even speak to me, Mom, because of my hair! Can you believe that?"

"Well, baby, sometimes people don't know how to respond to change. I know it hurts, but even when things change for us, sometimes so do the people around us and we have to be okay with that even if it means walking away from friendships. But we must always be willing to forgive those who hurt you in the process of having to let go."

The next day at school, when Kelly walked into her class, she noticed some of her classmates were now wearing their hair just like hers, including her new friend Olivia. All she could think about was her mom saying, "When you love yourself, you set the trends and people may laugh in the beginning but soon they will follow your lead." Kelly was greeted with laughter and joy as she complimented each of her new friends on their new braids.

Hailee soon approached Kelly and said, "Kelly, I'm so sorry for the way I acted yesterday. I guess I was just... I guess I was just... you know... jealous."

Kelly smiled. "Hailee, you don't have to be jealous of me or a hairstyle. My mom can do the same hairstyle for you too!"

"Can she really?"

"Sure, she can!" Hailee smiled the biggest smile Kelly had never seen before as they hugged before taking their seats just in time for class to begin.

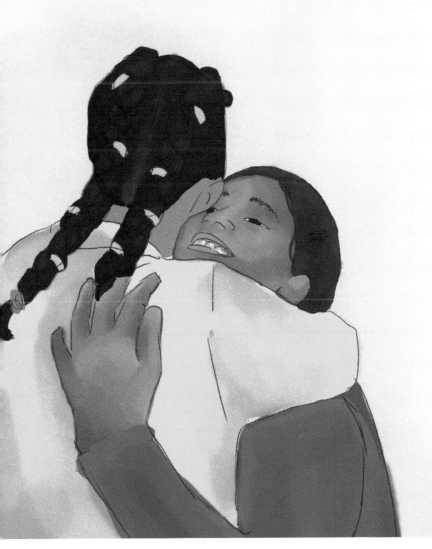

As Kelly sat down at her desk , she realized that a trend is only good if it inspires others to love themselves for who they truly are.

CPSIA information can be obtained
at www.ICGtesting.com
Printed in the USA
LVHW070747150821
695291LV00012B/795

9 780578 920542